TIMES & SEASONS

CLIP ART FOR THE LITURGICAL YEAR

ILLUSTRATIONS BY

PETER EDWARDS

McCRIMMONS

Great Wakering   Essex   England

Copying the art in this book

The art in this book may be copied freely **by the purchaser** for use in a parish, school or community. This art may not be used in any publications intended to be sold without prior permission from the publisher.

Times & Seasons
Clip Art for the Liturgical Year

First published 1993 by
McCrimmon Publishing Company Ltd.
10-12 High Street, Great Wakering, Essex, SS3 0EQ
Telephone (0702) 218956

Illustrations © 1993 Peter Edwards
Compilation & layout © 1993 McCrimmon Publishing Company Ltd

ISBN 0 85597 484 2

Cover design by Peter Edwards
Layout by Nick Snode
Printed by Island Press, Seaford, Sussex, England

CONTENTS

INTRODUCTION

This collection of over 300 pictures is the work of Essex artist and designer, Peter Edwards. They were originally produced for his local church. Now they are available for parishes, communities and schools to use in bulletins, worship leaflets and handouts of all kinds.

Illustrations are included for every Sunday of the three year cycle of the Roman Catholic lectionary. A cross reference is also included in order that they can be used by those churches which follow the two year ASB lectionary.

The pictures are not limited in their interpretation to only one occasion. This book provides a valuable resource for those who have the responsibility of preparing visual material for their community.

Most of the illustrations are reproduced twice, as experience suggests that often pictures are cut out of a collection and then cannot be traced when required again. The different sizes enable them to be used with the minimum of enlargement or reduction.

You are free to copy the art from this book without acknowledgement if you use the art for a parish, school or community. However, if you wish to sell any publication containing this art written permission of the publisher must be obtained.

Note

On many of the pages reference codes are included to assist in the location of a particular illustration. The code works as follows:

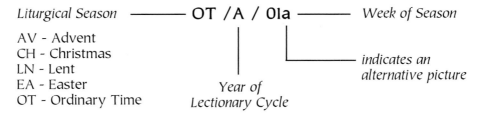

AV/A/03

AV/A/01

AV/A/02

AV/A/04

AV/B/01

AV/B/01a

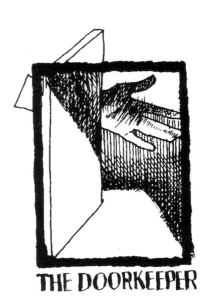

THE DOORKEEPER

THE DOORKEEPER

AV/B/02a

AV/B/02

AV/B/03

AV/B/04

AV/C/01a

AV/C/01

AV/C/01b

AV/C/02a

AV/C/02

AV/C/02b

AV/C/03

AV/ABC/03

AV/C/04

AV/C/04a

CH/C/02

CH/ABC/02

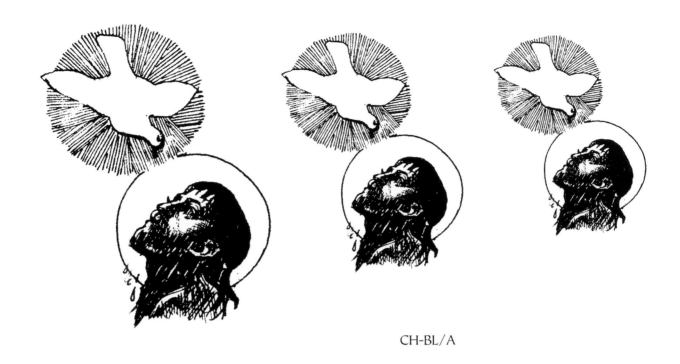

CH-BL/A

CH-BL/B

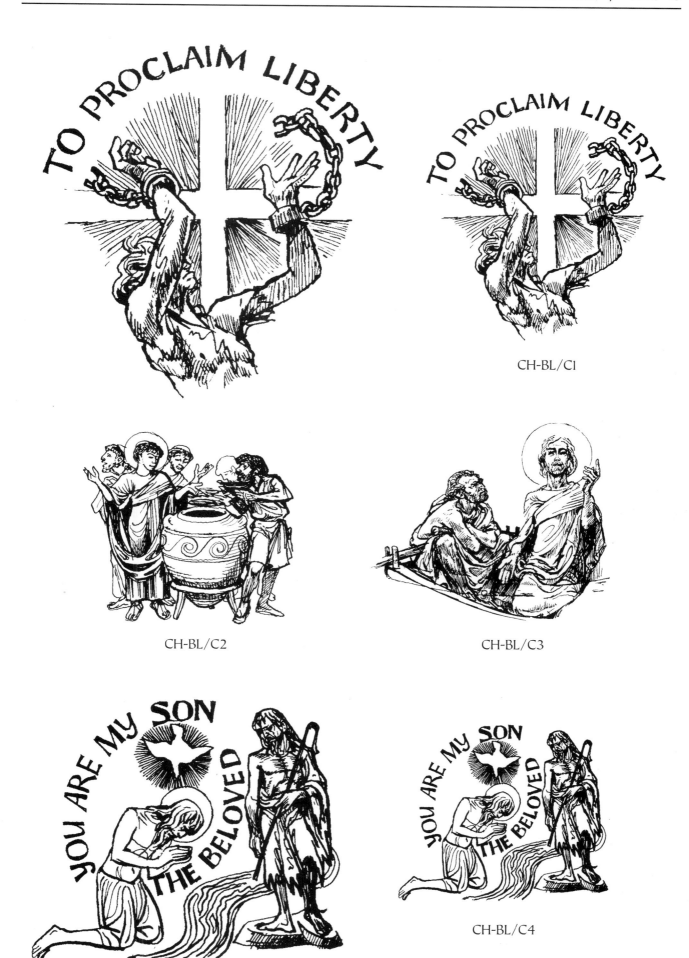

CH-BL/C1

CH-BL/C2

CH-BL/C3

CH-BL/C4

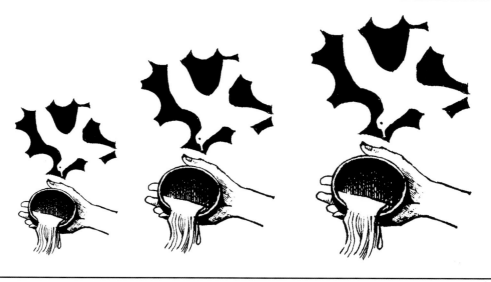

LN/A/01

LN/A/01a

LN/A/02

LN/A/03

LN/A/04

LN/A/05

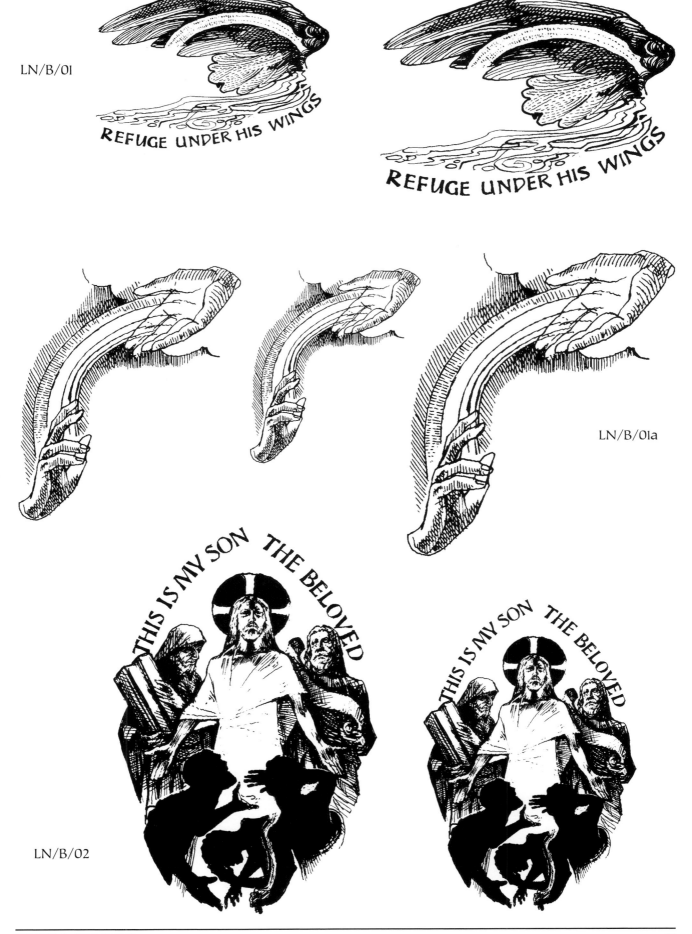

LN/B/01

REFUGE UNDER HIS WINGS

REFUGE UNDER HIS WINGS

LN/B/01a

LN/B/02

THIS IS MY SON THE BELOVED

THIS IS MY SON THE BELOVED

LN/B/02a

LN/B/02b

LN/B/03

LN/B/03a

LN/B/04

LN/B/04a

LN/B/05

LN/B/05a

LN/C/01a

LN/C/01

LN/C/02

LN/C/02a

LN/C/03

LN/C/03a

LN/C/04

LN/C/04a

LN/C/05

LN/C/05a

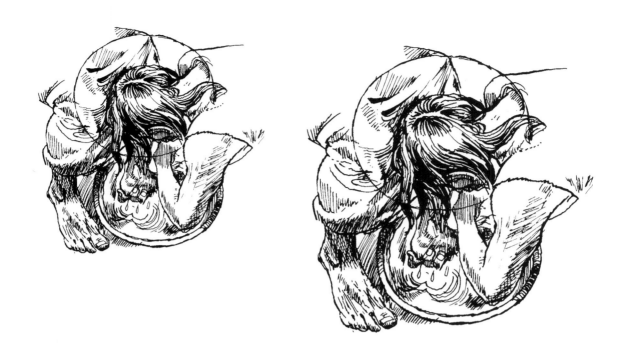

GOOD FRIDAY

EASTER VIGIL

EA/A/02

EA/A/03

EA/A/04

EA/A/05

EA/A/06

EA/A/07

EA/B/02

EA/B/02a

EA/B/03

EA/ABC/04

EA/ABC/04a

EA/ABC/04b

EA/B/05a

EA/B/05

EA/ABC/05

EA/B/06

EA/B/06a

EA/B/07

EA/B/07a

EA/C/02

EA/C/03

EA/C/04a

EA/C/04

EA/C/05

EA/C/06

EA/C/07

OT/A/02

OT/A/03

OT/A/03a

OT/A/04

OT/A/05

OT/A/05a

OT/A/06

OT/A/07

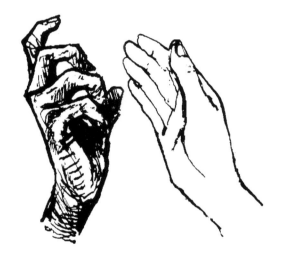

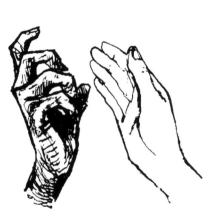

OT/A/08

OT/A/09

COME
JESUS
COME

COME
JESUS
COME

OT/A/10

OT/A/11

OT/A/12

OT/A/13

OT/A/14

OT/A/15

OT/A/16

OT/A/17

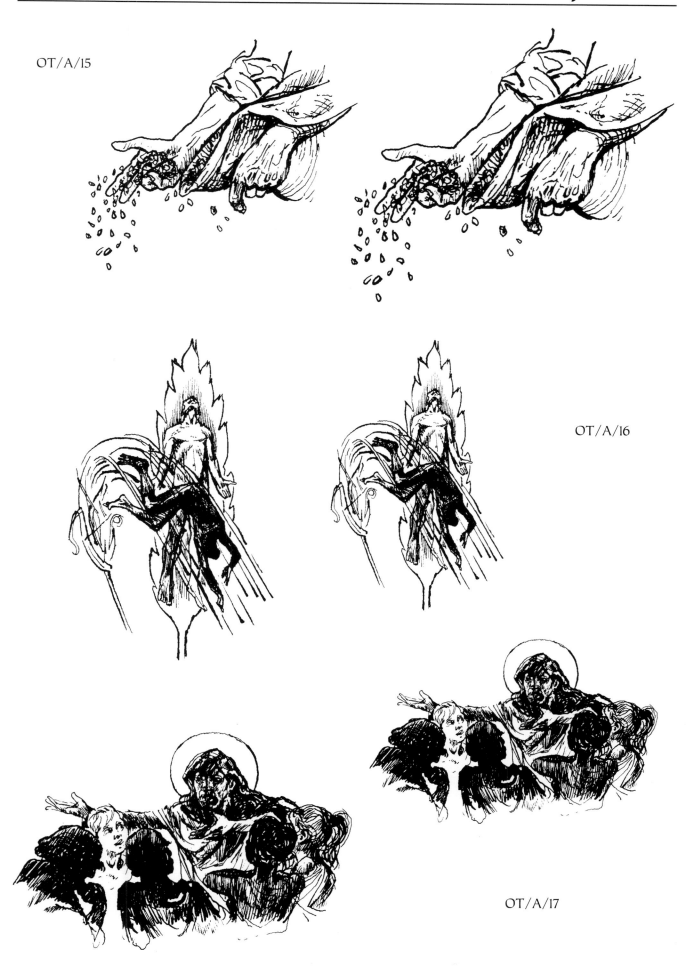

OT/A/18

OT/A/19

OT/A/20

OT/A/21

OT/A/22

OT/A/22a

OT/A/23

OT/A/24

OT/A/25

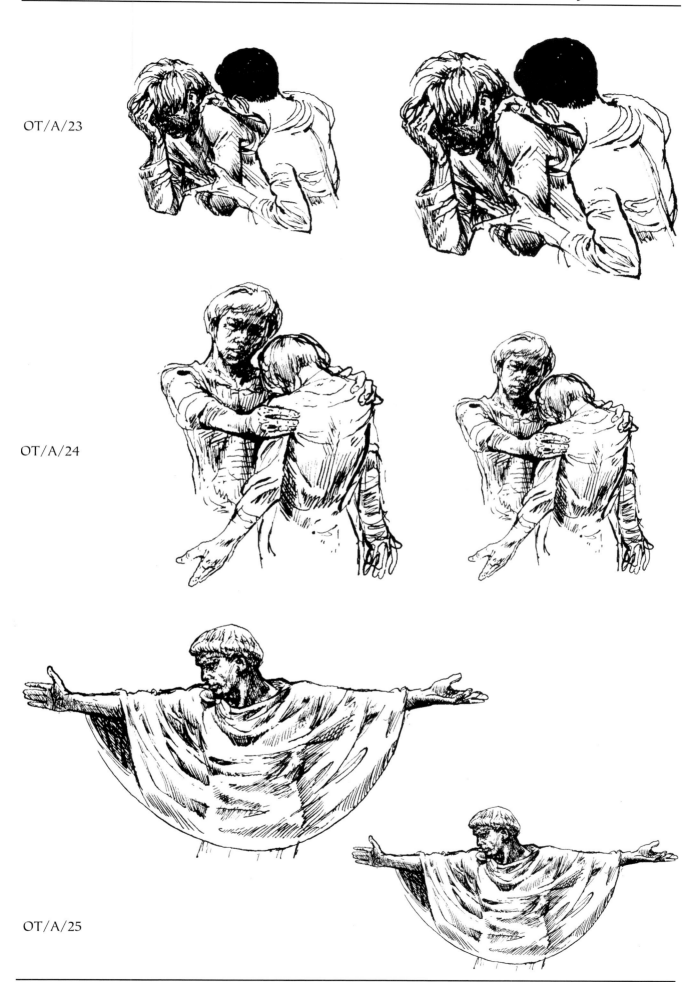

OT/A/26

THE LORD OF
THE VINEYARD

THE LORD OF
THE VINEYARD

OT/A/27

OT/A/28

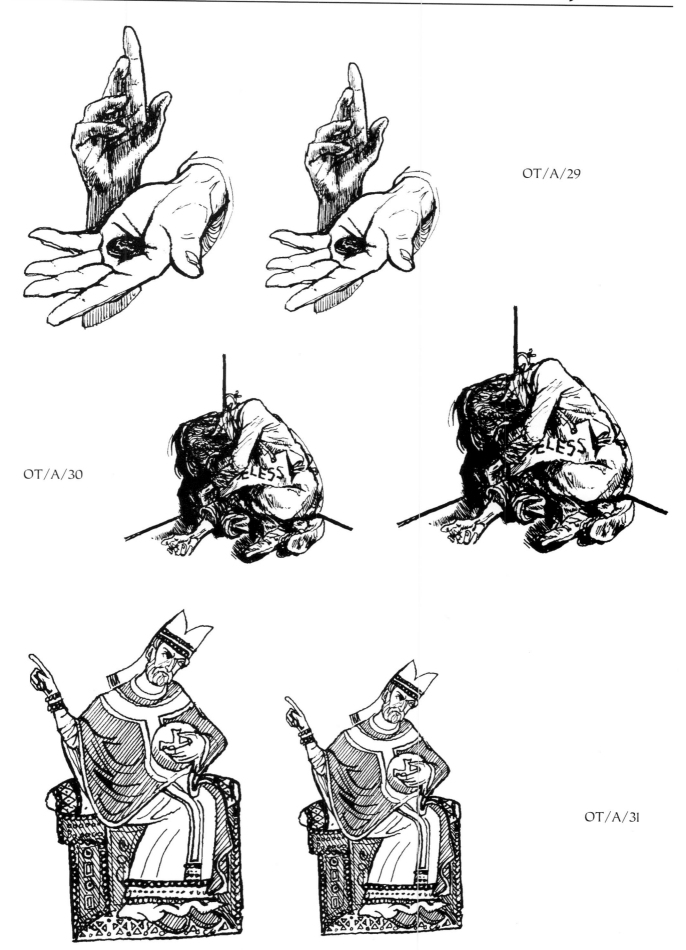

OT/A/29

OT/A/30

OT/A/31

OT/A/32

OT/A/33

OT/B/02

OT/B/02b

HERE I AM, LORD

HERE I AM, LORD

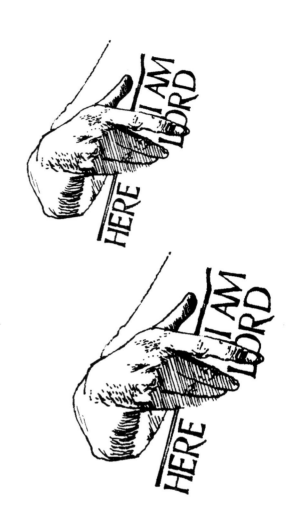

OT/B/03

OT/B/04

OT/B/05

BE CURED!

OT/B/06

BE CURED!

OT/B/07

OT/B/08

OT/B/09

OT/B/10

OT/B/11

OT/B/12

OT/B/12a

OT/B/13

OT/B/14

OT/B/15

OT/B/16

OT/B/17a

OT/B/17

OT/B/18

OT/B/19

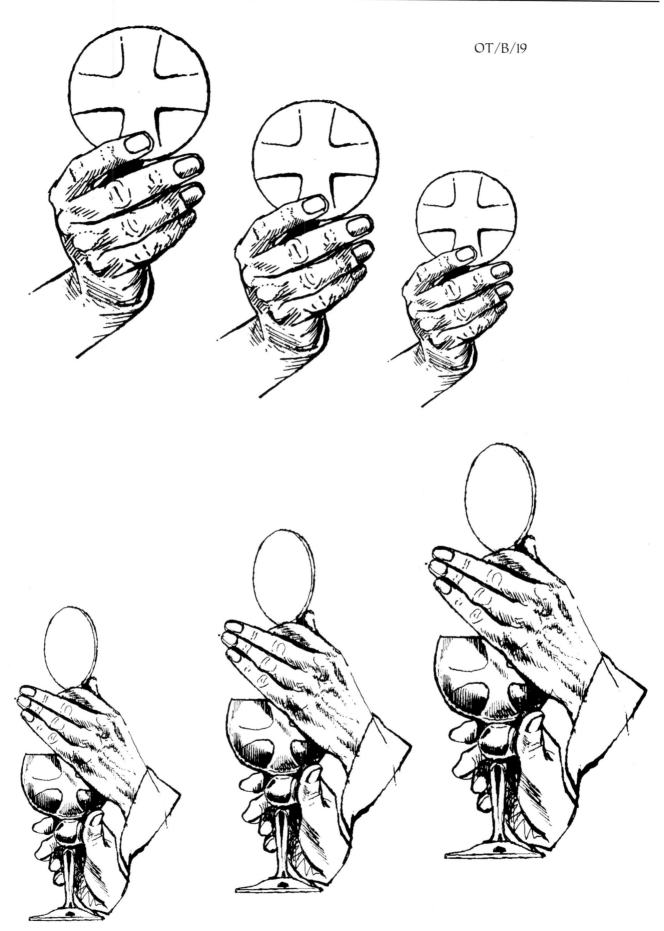

OT/B/20

OT/B/21

OT/B/22

OT/B/23

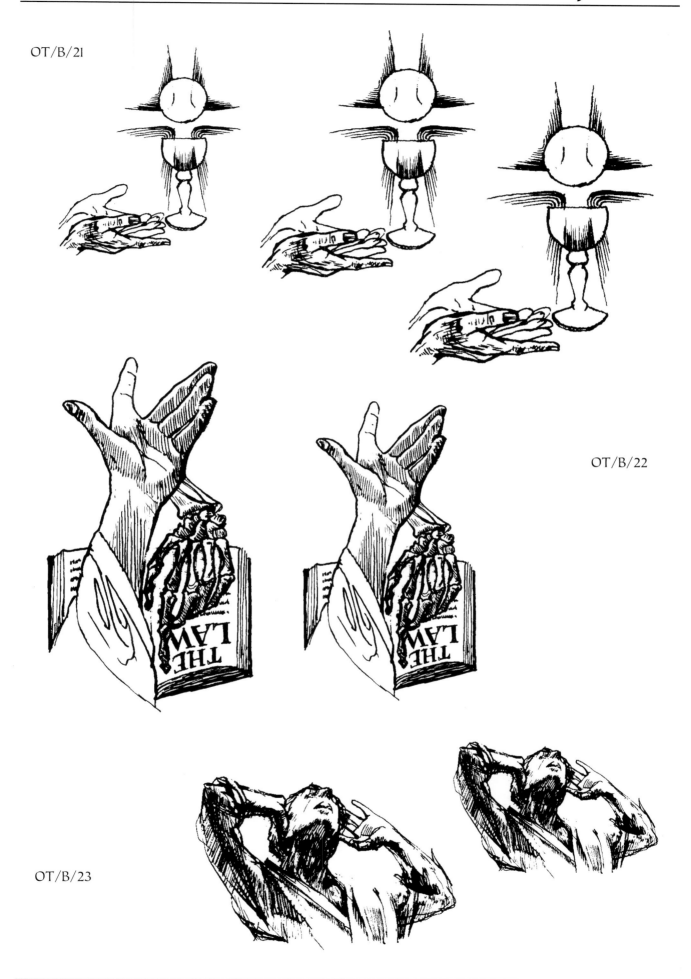

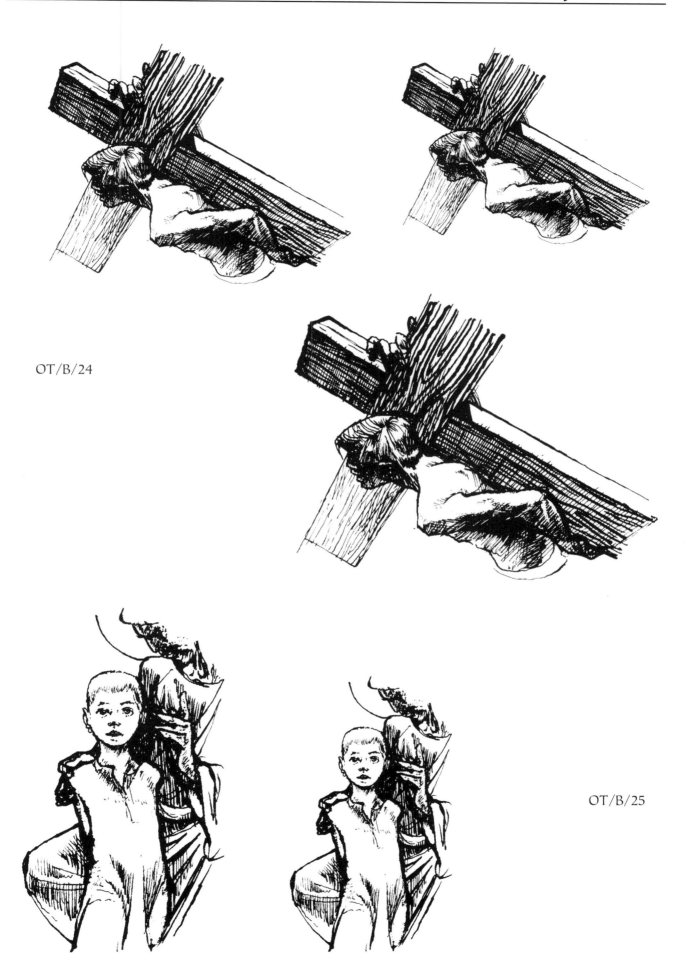

OT/B/24

OT/B/25

OT/B/26

OT/B/27

OT/B/28

OT/B/29

OT/B/30

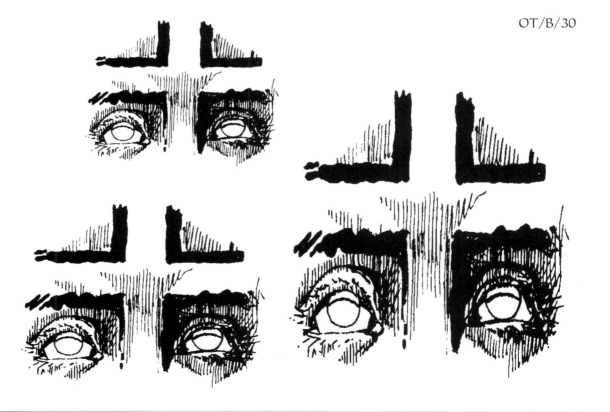

OT/B/31

OT/B/32

OT/B/33

OT/C/02

OT/C/03

OT/C/04

OT/C/05

OT/C/06

OT/C/07

OT/C/08

OT/C/09

OT/C/10

OT/C/11

OT/C/12

OT/C/13

OT/C/14

OT/C/15

THE WORD
IS VERY NEAR

THE WORD
IS VERY NEAR

IT IS MARY
WHO HAS
CHOSEN THE
BETTER WAY

IT IS MARY
WHO HAS
CHOSEN THE
BETTER WAY

OT/C/16

OT/C/17

OT/C/17a

OT/C/19

OT/C/18

OT/C/19a

OT/C/20

OT/C/21

OT/C/22

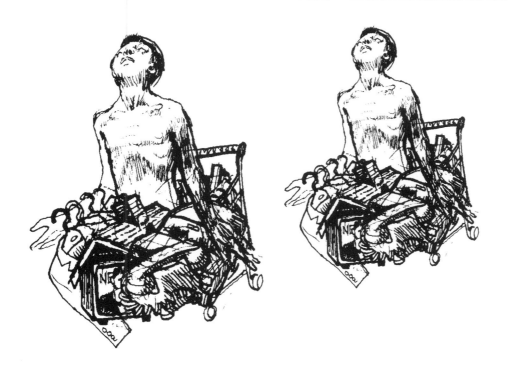

OT/C/23

OT/C/24

OT/C/24a

OT/C/25

OT/C/26

OT/C/26a

OT/C/27

OT/C/28

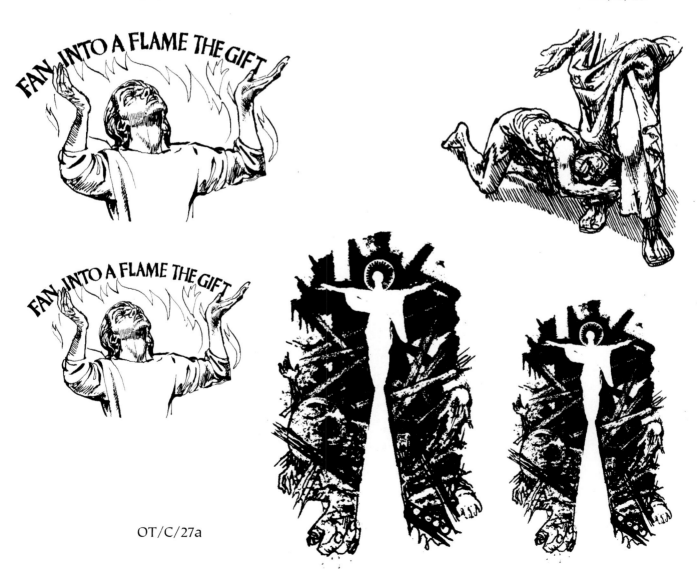

OT/C/27a

OT/C/29

OT/C/30a

OT/C/30

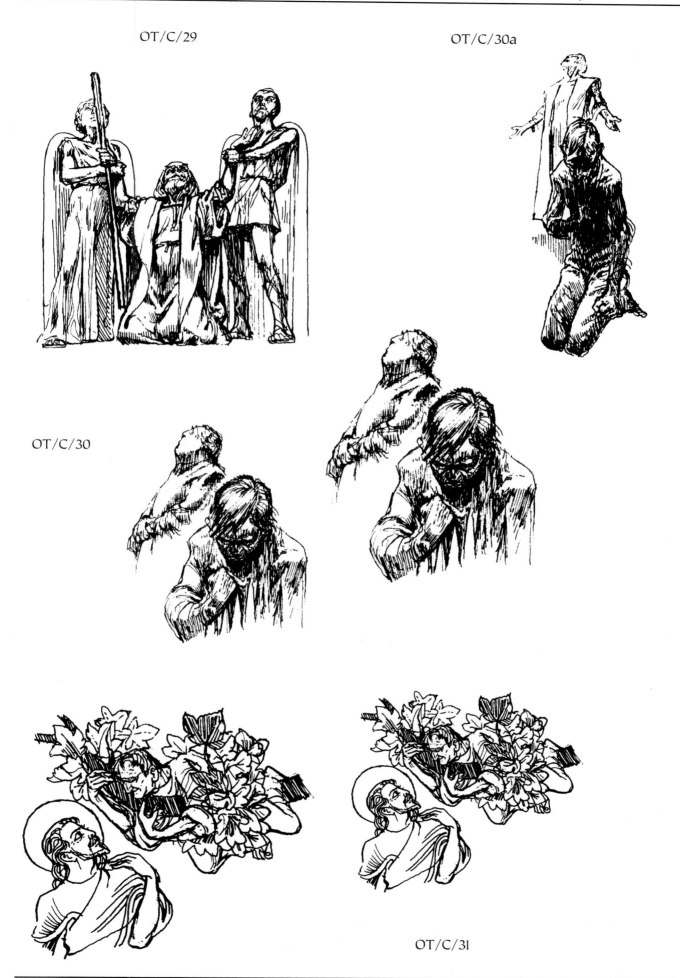

OT/C/31

OT/C/32

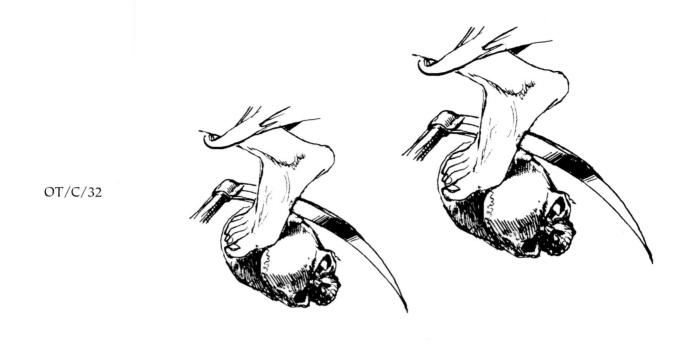

OT/C/33

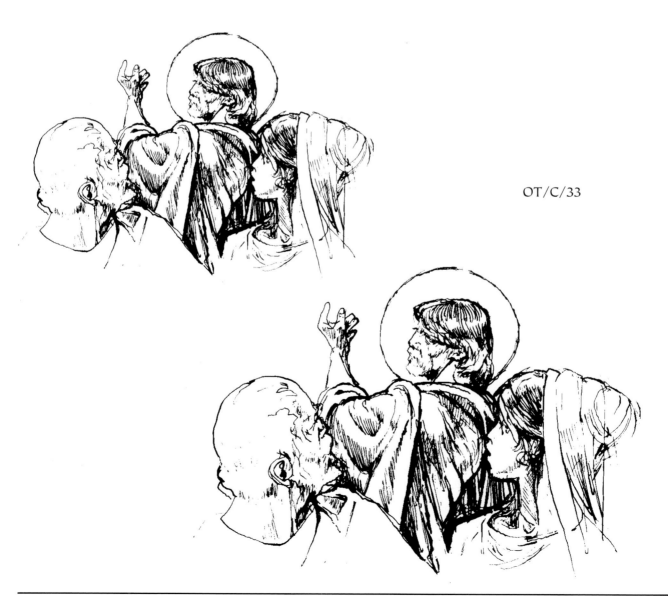

HOLY DAYS & FEASTS / *Transfiguration* / *August 6th*

HOLY DAYS & FEASTS / *All Saints*

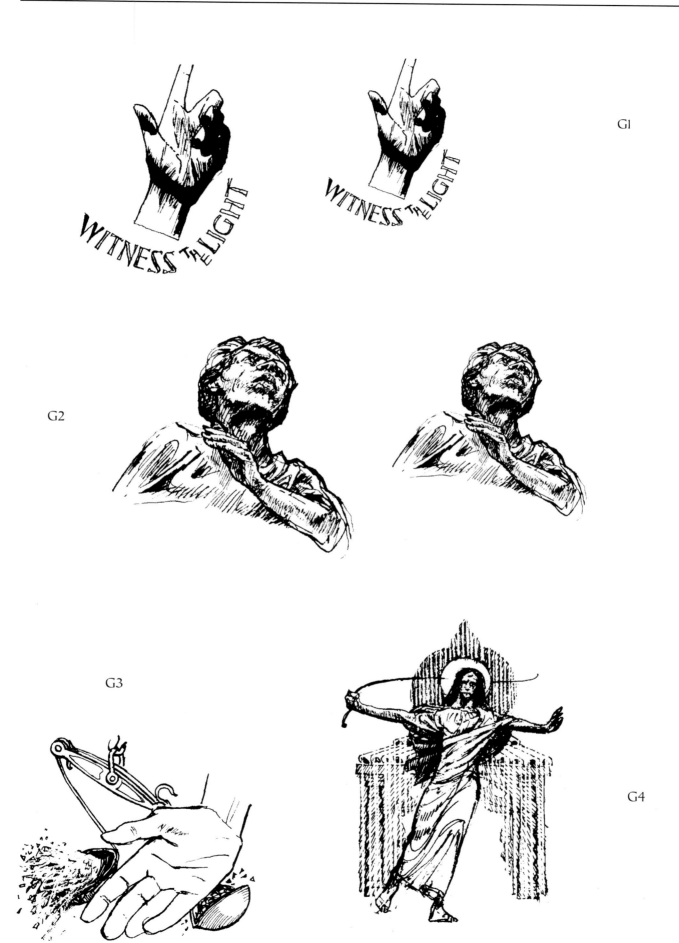

G1

G2

G3

G4

G5

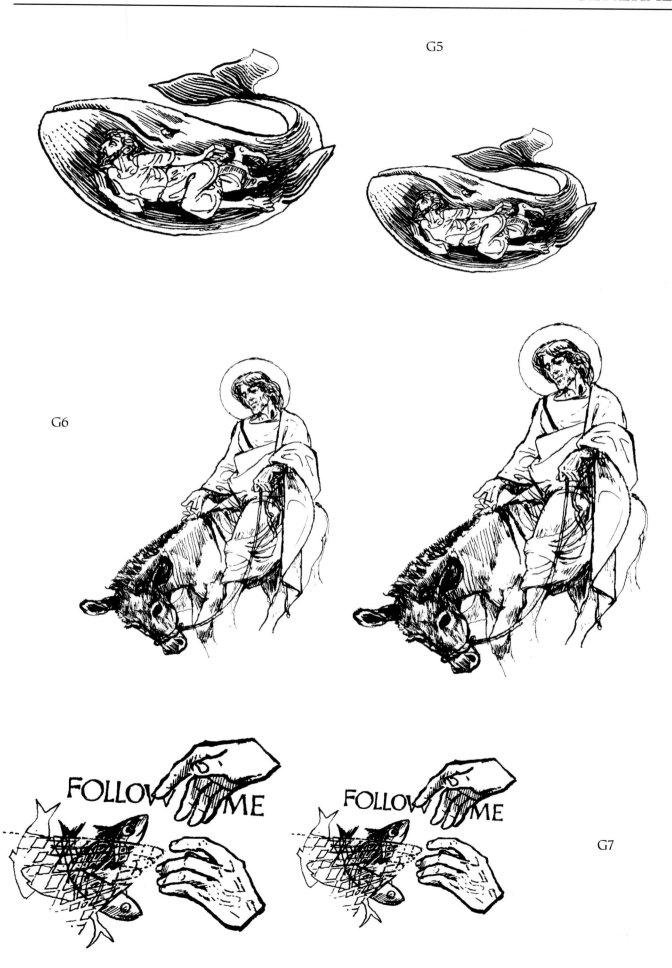

G6

G7

G8

G9

G10

Gll

Gl2

Gl3

G14

G15

G16

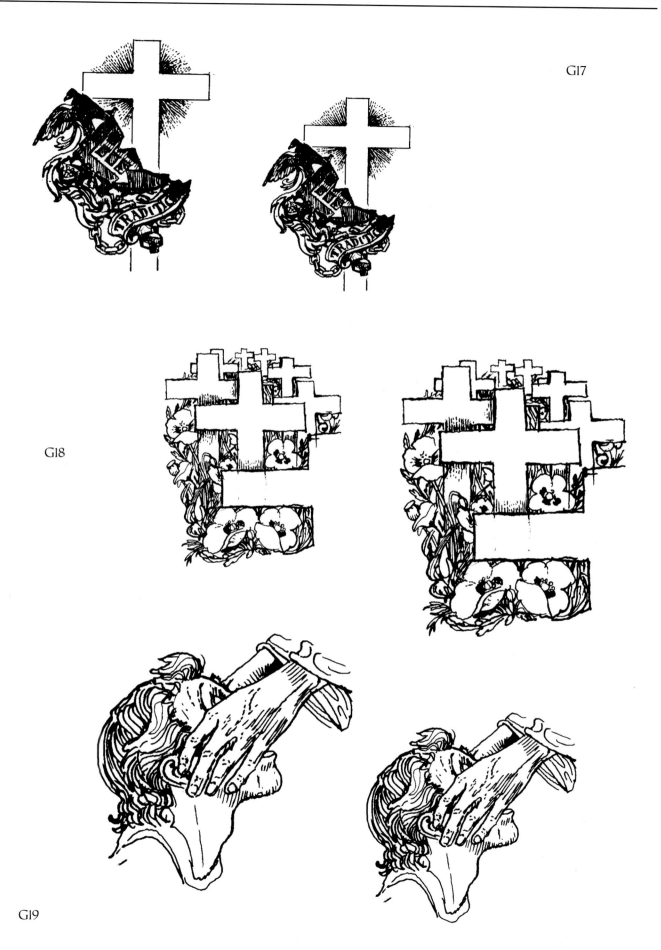

G17

G18

G19

G20

G21

G22

IF IT DIES
IT YIELDS
A RICH
HARVEST

G23

G24

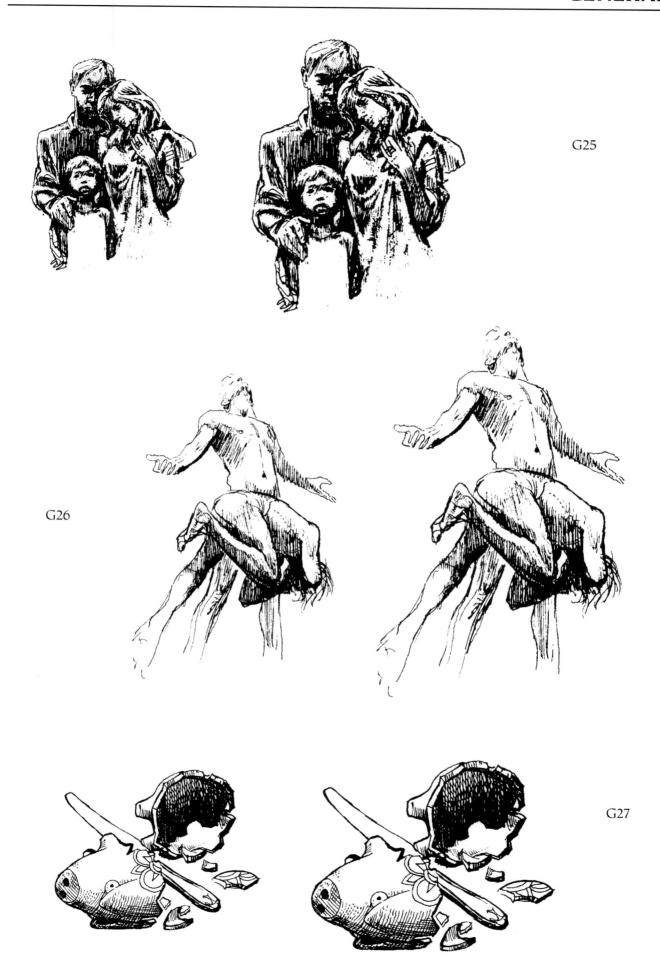

G25

G26

G27

G28

G29

G30

G31

G32

G33

G34

G35

G36

G37

G38

G39

MATTHEW

XT THE MAN

G40

MARK

XT IN KINGSHIP

G41

LUKE

XT THE SACRIFICE

G42

JOHN

XT SOARS TO HEAVEN

G43

INDEXES

INDEX 1 3 year Lectionary cycle

	Year A	Year B	Year C
1st Sunday of Advent	1	2	4
2nd Sunday of Advent	1	2	4, 5
3rd Sunday of Advent	1, 6	3, 6	5, 6
4th Sunday of Advent	1	3	6
Christmas Day	7	7	7
The Holy Family	8, 9	8, 9	8, 9
2nd Sunday after Christmas	10	10	10
Epiphany	11, 12	11, 12	11, 12
The Baptism of the Lord	13, 15	13, 15	14, 15
Presentation of the Lord	15	15	15
1st Sunday of Lent	16	18	22
2nd Sunday of Lent	16	18, 19	22, 23
3rd Sunday of Lent	17	19, 20	23
4th Sunday of Lent	17	20	24
5th Sunday of Lent	17	21	25
Passion/Palm Sunday	26, 27	26, 27	26, 27
Holy Thursday	28	28	28
Good Friday	28, 29	28, 29	28, 29
Easter Vigil	29	29	29
Easter Sunday	30, 31	30, 31	30, 31
2nd Sunday of Easter	32	34	39
3rd Sunday of Easter	32	34	39
4th Sunday of Easter	32	35	39
5th Sunday of Easter	33, 36	36	36, 40
6th Sunday of Easter	33	37	40
7th Sunday of Easter	33	38	40
Ascension	41	41	41
Pentecost	42, 43	42, 43	42, 43
Trinity Sunday	44	44	42
2nd Sunday in Ordinary Time	45	57	70
3rd Sunday in Ordinary Time	45	57	70
4th Sunday in Ordinary Time	46	58	70
5th Sunday in Ordinary Time	46	58	71
6th Sunday in Ordinary Time	47	59	71

INDEX 1

	Year A	Year B	Year C
7th Sunday in Ordinary Time	47	59	71
8th Sunday in Ordinary Time	47	59	72
9th Sunday in Ordinary Time	48	60	72
10th Sunday in Ordinary Time	48	60	72
11th Sunday in Ordinary Time	48	60	73
12th Sunday in Ordinary Time	49	61	73
13th Sunday in Ordinary Time	49	61	73
14th Sunday in Ordinary Time	49	62	74
15th Sunday in Ordinary Time	50	62	74
16th Sunday in Ordinary Time	50	62	74
17th Sunday in Ordinary Time	50	63	75
18th Sunday in Ordinary Time	51	63	75
19th Sunday in Ordinary Time	51	64	75
20th Sunday in Ordinary Time	51	64	76
21st Sunday in Ordinary Time	52	65	76
22nd Sunday in Ordinary Time	52	65	76
23rd Sunday in Ordinary Time	53	65	77
24th Sunday in Ordinary Time	53	66	77
25th Sunday in Ordinary Time	53	66	77
26th Sunday in Ordinary Time	54	67	78
27th Sunday in Ordinary Time	54	67	78
28th Sunday in Ordinary Time	54	68	78
29th Sunday in Ordinary Time	55	68	79
30th Sunday in Ordinary Time	55	68	79
31st Sunday in Ordinary Time	55	69	79
32nd Sunday in Ordinary Time	56	69	80
33rd Sunday in Ordinary Time	56	69	80
Christ the King	81, 82	81, 82	81, 82
John the Baptist	83	83	83
Ss Peter & Paul, Apostles	83	83	83
Corpus Christi	84	84	84
The Transfiguration	84	84	84
All Saints	84	84	84

INDEX 2   2 year Lectionary cycle

	Year 1	Year 2
9th Sunday before Christmas	7	7
8th Sunday before Christmas	6	20
7th Sunday before Christmas	87	55
6th Sunday before Christmas	63	80
5th Sunday before Christmas	2	87
Advent Sunday	4	81, 82
Advent 2	87	62
Advent 3	3, 6	1, 6
Advent 4	3	1
Christmas Eve	7	7
Christmas Day	7	7
Sunday after Christmas Day	7	7
2nd Sunday after Christmas	8, 9	8, 9
Epiphany of Our Lord	11, 12	11, 12
Epiphany 1	13, 15	45
Epiphany 2	57	57
Epiphany 3	57	63
Epiphany 4	19, 20	17
Epiphany 5	86	86
Epiphany 6	50	50
9th Sunday before Easter	46	84
8th Sunday before Easter	59	65
7th Sunday before Easter	48	25
Lent 1	16	22
Lent 2	19, 20	60
Lent 3	73	52
Lent 4	22, 23	84
Lent 5	21	68
Palm Sunday	26, 27	26, 27
Maundy Thursday	28	28
Good Friday	28, 29	28, 29
Easter Eve	29	29
Easter Day	30, 31	30, 31
Easter 1	32	63

	Year 1	Year 2
Easter 2	32	35
Easter 3	39	17
Easter 4	83	33, 36
Easter 5	96	84
Ascension Day	41	41
Sunday after Ascension	41	41
Pentecost	42, 43	42, 43
Trinity Sunday	44	44
2nd Sunday after Pentecost	36	54
3rd Sunday after Pentecost	37	61
4th Sunday after Pentecost	37	77
5th Sunday after Pentecost	68	74
6th Sunday after Pentecost	77	68
7th Sunday after Pentecost	53	69
8th Sunday after Pentecost	42, 43	71
9th Sunday after Pentecost	38	93
10th Sunday after Pentecost	28	73
11th Sunday after Pentecost	36, 40	53
12th Sunday after Pentecost	40	46
13th Sunday after Pentecost	87	80
14th Sunday after Pentecost	67	75
15th Sunday after Pentecost	55	92
16th Sunday after Pentecost	74	78
17th Sunday after Pentecost	78	72
18th Sunday after Pentecost	47	56
19th Sunday after Pentecost	47	80
20th Sunday after Pentecost	73	48
21st Sunday after Pentecost	79	17
22nd Sunday after Pentecost	77	77
Last Sunday after Pentecost	33	56